Plus

Asian Animals

Bengal Tigers

by Lyn A. Sirota

Consulting Editor: Gail Saunders-Smith, PhD

Content Consultant: Tanya Dewey, PhD
University of Michigan Museum of Zoology

CAPSTONE PRESS
a capstone imprint

Pebble Plus is published by Capstone Press,
151 Good Counsel Drive, P.O. Box 669, Mankato, Minnesota 56002.
www.capstonepress.com

092009
005618CGS10

Books published by Capstone Press are manufactured with paper
containing at least 10 percent post-consumer waste.

Library of Congress Cataloging-in-Publication Data
Sirota, Lyn A., 1963–
    Bengal tigers / by Lyn A. Sirota.
    p. cm. — (Pebble plus. Asian animals)
    Summary: "Simple text and photographs present Bengal tigers, how they look, where they live, and what
they do" — Provided by publisher.
    Includes bibliographical references and index.
    ISBN 978-1-4296-4032-9 (library binding)
    ISBN 978-1-4296-4843-1 (paperback)
    1. Tigers — Juvenile literature. I. Title.
QL737.C23.S5626 2010
599.756 — dc22   2009028640

Editorial Credits
Katy Kudela, editor; Matt Bruning, designer; Svetlana Zhurkin, media researcher; Eric Manske, production specialist

Photo Credits
Alamy/Indian Gypsy, 15; Getty Images/The Image Bank/Anup Shah, 11; Getty Images/Photographer's Choice/
James Warwick, 21; Getty Images/Photolibrary/Richard Packwood, cover; Getty Images/Photonica/Theo Allofs, 7;
iStockphoto/Mark Kostich, 1; Minden Pictures/Theo Allofs, 17; Nature Picture Library/E. A. Kuttapan, 9;
Peter Arnold/Wildlife, 5; Photoshot/Bruce Coleman/Tom Brakefield, 19; Shutterstock/Chris Sargent, 13

Note to Parents and Teachers

The Asian Animals series supports national science standards related to life science. This book
describes and illustrates Bengal tigers. The images support early readers in understanding
the text. The repetition of words and phrases helps early readers learn new words. This book
also introduces early readers to subject-specific vocabulary words, which are defined in the
Glossary section. Early readers may need assistance to read some words and to use the Table of
Contents, Glossary, Read More, Internet Sites, and Index sections of the book.

Table of Contents

Living in Asia

Bengal tigers roam the grass, swamps, and forests of Asia. These large cats hunt at night.

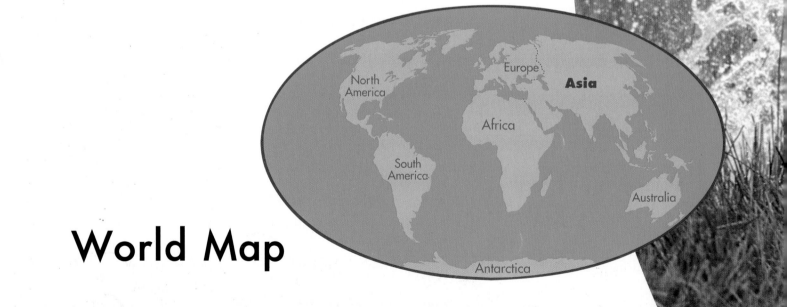

World Map

Days in southern Asia
are steamy and hot.
Tigers rest in dens
or swim in rivers
to stay cool.

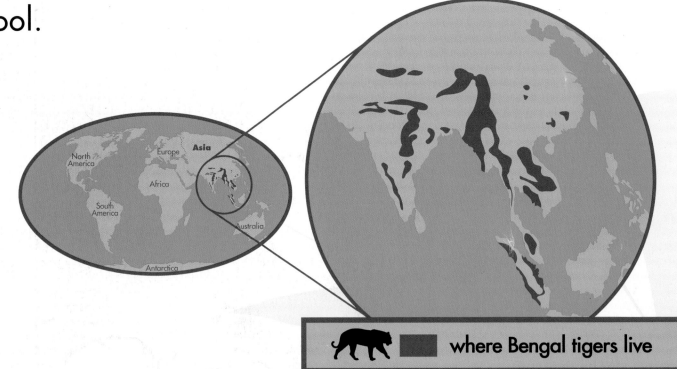

where Bengal tigers live

Up Close!

Each tiger's coat has

a different pattern of stripes.

Stripes hide a tiger

in tall grass.

Tigers walk quietly
on padded paws.
They pull in their claws
to keep the claws
from wearing down.

Bengals are mighty predators.

They have sharp teeth

and strong jaws

to grab prey.

Hunting

A tiger hunts alone

and follows its prey.

Then it springs.

Hungry tigers hunt
deer, buffalo, and wild pigs.
A tiger can eat 40 pounds
(18 kilograms) of meat
in one meal.

Staying Safe

A mother tiger
keeps her cubs safe.
She stays close to her cubs
when hunting.

Bengals are endangered.

They have few places to hunt.

People have set aside

safe places for tigers to live.

Glossary

claw — a hard, curved nail on the feet of some animals

coat — an animal's hair or fur

cub — a young tiger

den — a place where a wild animal lives

endangered — in danger of dying out

pattern — a repeating order of colors and shapes

predator — an animal that hunts other animals for food

prey — an animal hunted by another animal for food

roam — to travel across a large area

swamp — an area of wet, spongy ground with lots of plants

Read More

Scheunemann, Pam. *Tigers Roar*! Animal Sounds. Edina, Minn.: Abdo, 2009.

Spilsbury, Louise, and Richard Spilsbury. *Bengal Tiger*. Save Our Animals! Chicago: Heinemann, 2006.

Suen, Anastasia. *A Tiger Grows Up*. Wild Animals. Minneapolis: Picture Window Books, 2006.

Internet Sites

FactHound offers a safe, fun way to find Internet sites related to this book. All of the sites on FactHound have been researched by our staff.

Here's all you do:

Visit *www.facthound.com*

FactHound will fetch the best sites for you!

Index

Word Count: 149
Grade: 1
Early-Intervention Level: 18